PRAYER
BOOK

PRAYER
BOOK

DISCOVER YOUR SPIRITUAL SELF
THROUGH PRAYER

Alan Walker

 A GODSFIELD BOOK

First published in Great Britain in 2003
by Godsfield Press Ltd,
Laurel House, Station Approach, Alresford
Hampshire SO24 9JH, U.K.

10 9 8 7 6 5 4 3 2 1

Designed and produced for Godsfield Press by
The Bridgewater Book Company

Printed and bound in China

ISBN 1-84181-161-0

Cover photography: Tony Stone (prayer beads picture).

CONTENTS

TUNING IN TO SOMETHING GREATER

E WANT to pray because we sense that we are more than material beings living only for the present. Whatever our background or beliefs, we believe that our lives are part of something greater than this everyday existence.

There are times when we become particularly aware of our place in the universe. These may not be moments of great revelation, but they take us beyond ourselves and connect us to something more than ourselves. A beautiful piece of music, a sublime sunset, or an experience of tenderness can fill us with the urge to say "thank you" for the gifts that life brings. And then when things are not going so well for us, when life feels harsh or we are facing trouble or loss, or when we long for support and comfort, we experience, through the care and comfort that others give us, the compassion that is at the heart of the universe.

These moments of insight, when it seems as though the scales have fallen from our eyes and we can see clearly our bond to all that is, are some of the most important experiences of our lives. They remind us who and what we really are. They are cherished clues to our sacred identity. The various religious traditions of the world use different words to describe our nature and destiny, but they all agree that regardless of background, education, or circumstances we each have the power to tune in to the mystery underlying existence. *Tuning in* is at the root of prayer, enabling us to move beyond ourselves into the sacred realm.

We may express this tuning in in different ways: as the soul entering into communion with God; as the individual experiencing a sense of profound identity with the human or the natural world; as a perception of the ultimate

unreality of everything that keeps us focused on ourselves. Whatever our understanding of prayer might be, we understand it as an attempt to reestablish communication as the primary characteristic of the cosmos. Prayer is the energy that draws the disparate elements of our world together in conversation and empowers us to live in the world as spiritual beings.

To live a life of prayer, then, is to live more fully than we ordinarily do. It is to live with our whole selves and not just a part of our selves. A person who is praying does not reject or exclude the material parts of human nature, but seeks to restore these to a more balanced place in life as a whole. If prayer begins with the understanding that the eternal is not alien or unknown to us, it continues with the insight that the eternal does not oppress or destroy us.

For many of us, prayer is something we turn to when we feel unable to cope or when we need to enlist resources that go beyond what we believe to be within us. Prayer also beckons when we need to get something off our chests or come to terms with the past. Most of us have experienced wanting to shout with joy in gratitude for an achievement or good fortune we never expected and hardly believe we deserve. Each of these expressions can be seen as a kind of prayer when it takes us out of ourselves.

Prayer has been called a journey. In the modern world, more and more people have the opportunity to travel and investigate far-off places and cultures. Many are challenged by the possibilities of endurance and adventure

in sport and exploration. Others are excited by the infinite possibilities of literature, art, and music. Whatever our enthusiasms and abilities, through them we can sense what it must mean to receive the mystical call. Prayer is about allowing our lives to become infused with eternity.

In this book we explore ways to rediscover our spiritual nature, not as an intellectual exercise but as an act of memory in which we recall what we have already glimpsed. This book is intended to be a practical introduction to prayer and ways of praying. It draws on the insights and experiences of members of many traditions—the great world religions, ancient wisdom, and contemporary spiritualities—and seeks to interpret and present them for those who already belong to a faith community, those whose personal quest has not brought them to any formal allegiance, and those who feel constrained or uneasy with the religion of their childhood. It presents techniques that can help each of us to deepen our spirituality.

We will go on a journey into prayer that follows the natural rhythms and movements of life. We have already had many experiences of prayer in our lives: childhood trust and joy, the trials of growing up and finding our own sense of identity and place in the world, taking responsibility for others, and coping with loss and disappointment. All of these ordinary human experiences can be starting points for prayer and link us to the spiritual world of the great masters and mystics of the world traditions. We shall see that they are not so different from us as we learn to identify and develop our own spiritual natures on our common journey from the cradle to the grave. Prayers from the world traditions have helped many people through difficult times and enabled them to celebrate happier ones. We will explore these traditions and look at ways to give expression to our own spiritual thoughts.

As we will discover, prayer is a natural expression of what it means to be alive in our world. Prayer springs from the heart in what has traditionally been called praise, confession, concern, meditation, and contemplation. In praise we express our thanks for being here and being privileged to experience the beauty and joy of the world. Those happy thoughts also let us understand how

we have not done all we might to contribute to the world and sometimes we feel the need to confess our sense of failure and admit to our negative actions. The natural progress of our deepening spirituality reminds us that we cannot be entirely to blame for all we feel guilty about. We belong to communities and systems that make us what we are. It is through working positively within those that we are drawn beyond our gloomier thoughts. Our concern for others liberates us from our past. We find, through accepting responsibility, a new sense of peace that allows us to continue our journey. In meditation we use the experiences of those preserved in the traditions to go deeper into ourselves. We follow and identify with their journeys as we move into contemplation, a personal communion with the divine ground of our being and of all there is—the goal of our pilgrimage.

This book is for everyone who wants to live life more fully through developing the spiritual potential that belongs to all of us. We may come to prayer initially because we are in joy or despair, but we come always because prayer is natural. The desire for more is built into us. We may have tried prayer before but been confused by technical terms and demanding and impersonal doctrines, or by the belief that we have to conform to prescribed ways of talking about or doing things. This book takes us behind these externals to the place where human and divine meet.

PART ONE

THE NATURE OF PRAYER

PRAYER AND RELIGION

ALTHOUGH all of us are spiritual beings, we each express our spirituality in different ways. We differ from one another in terms of strength, talent, and general ability. Indeed, we differ from ourselves in many ways over the course of our lives, peaking in different skills and abilities at particular times and ages.

The great religious traditions of the world emerged before the age of the individual. They can be thought of as blueprints for the spiritual life, but as a general application, not tailored to the needs of any individual. Over the centuries many movements sprang up within the traditions to meet local and personal needs. Some of these won approval—usually after a period of suspicion—and became part of the mainstream "schools" within the greater movement. Others did not achieve recognition and found themselves marginalized as "sects" unless and until they were able to grow into separate traditions of their own. In this way, Christianity emerged out of Judaism, and Buddhism out of what later came to be called Hinduism.

Viewed historically, the emergence of these new traditions is usually explained in terms of doctrinal controversies or social and economic factors. Their development may also be accounted for as an expansion in the number of spiritual possibilities available to humankind. The original design did not meet the needs of some practitioners who wanted to emphasize certain doctrines or practices rather than those more officially highlighted.

Unfortunately, until the modern era such modifications of tradition tended to turn into orthodoxies and tried to make people conform once again to unsuitable spiritual ways. Only recently have we realized that diversification does not have to mean the suppression of alternatives.

Each individual is different and the more this can be acknowledged within the traditions the healthier such traditions will become.

We have learned from modern psychology that there are different personality types and that individuals will interpret and respond to situations in different ways. Much effort has been spent making links between types and subtypes and between different ways of praying.

Different religions may suit some rather than others and conversion may be a sign of loyalty to faith in an increasingly secular society rather than of betrayal of an inherited world view. Fortunately, the more we learn about the great traditions—especially the ones we have been born into—the more we find that behind the official teachings are many different schools of expression.

The contemporary period is sometimes characterized as ungodly or irreligious, yet one of its most distinctive features, namely the fact that it is an age of travel, also makes it the greatest epoch of spiritual opportunity. Until a century ago most people spent their lives in the places where they were born. Their spiritual needs could usually be met only by the single religious institution in their locality—or by an alternative denomination perceived to be completely different but in reality only a variation on the same theme. Anyone who wanted to go deeper in faith would probably be encouraged to follow a prescribed route to which they had to conform. The image of the spiritual guide was of an otherworldly figure dictating rules to the disciple.

Today, travel and migration mean that genuine alternatives exist on our doorsteps—or at least within easy range—and, of course, increasingly through our computers. We can explore these options to find ways of living spiritually that suit our personalities and personal histories. Some of us will be called to an active life of prayer that is closely linked to improving conditions in the world. Others will be attracted by a more reflective approach that is no less concerned for others but that accepts individual limitations.

The word *attracted* is the important one. The divine is that which we most desire. It fascinates us and allures us. Yet at every stage we may be unwilling or afraid to submit to its charm. When it comes to identifying appropriate methods and practices in prayer, once we have embarked on the spiritual path and are making progress through observable changes in our lives, we can choose on the basis of what feels right for us at that moment. There is no point in forcing ourselves to pray in ways that mean nothing to us or have negative associations for us.

ENCOUNTERING THE MYSTERY

*P*RAYER is an encounter with the mystery underlying the universe: the world spirit, the divine, that reality that transcends the differences between humans and differences between humans and other living beings. We call this ultimate reality a mystery because we cannot grasp it with our minds, conceptualize it in our thoughts, or find adequate words to express it in language. We each need to find our own representation of the divine and be open to the need to revise and refine that image.

The sacred is not unknown to us. Throughout our lives we have been struggling either to keep the divine out of our lives or to take more account of the sacred character of human existence. Perhaps we were brought up in a religious faith with definite teachings about the nature of the divine. We may find that these teachings continue to meet our personal needs, but we are aware that in the modern world people have different or contradictory views. Our own convictions drive us to a greater appreciation of those of others. Can we learn from them or must we close ourselves off from what is unfamiliar?

Or perhaps we were not raised within an explicit belief system. We feel "there is something there," but we do not know how to construct a faith or we are unsure if that is what we should be doing at all. We have turned to this book because we are questioning. We are drawn with our minds because we are moved in our spirits or souls. If we acknowledge the sacred character of the universe and believe that we are most truly alive when we are in communication with the sacred, we have already begun to pray.

We begin our journey by recognizing that we have already made a start. There are no application forms to complete, no need—or time—to put things in order. When we identify the desire to pray we become aware of the urgency.

Today we understand that there is more to communication than speech. We are aware of the role of gestures, facial expressions, and other signs in communicating our thoughts and feelings to others. Prayer, too, is more than talk. It is obvious that merely "saying our prayers" hardly amounts to a human–divine encounter any more than some of the affectionate words we use every day really signal a genuine concern for our neighbors. Our words need the support of our emotions if they are to convey more than just information. They need to come from the heart as well as the lips. So we could say, echoing the words of the mystics of the eastern Christian Church, that

prayer is the language of the heart. It is the only really true language because sound and intention are completely in harmony.

When we were children we learned to speak by imitating the sounds that we heard and discovering the way they referred to the world all around us. Prayer begins with imitation and, if we allow it, proceeds with an ever-expanding relevance to our lives. We can speak because we have been spoken to. We can pray because we have already been touched by the divine.

The hardest thing always is to begin. Because we cannot conceptualize the holy, our encounters are always going to be "mediated"; that is, they are going to present themselves to us through other events and not necessarily extra-ordinary ones. What is extraordinary about the divine encounter is that it may come in the most mundane of circumstances.

But as we begin we turn to special moments to rediscover our sense of the sacred, our awareness of the presence of the holy. A piece of music or a set of words can take us "beyond ourselves." Certain places can seem to evoke and convey a sense of otherworldliness: a spectacular landscape reflects the majesty of creation; an old church or temple seems to have absorbed the prayers of generations of worshipers in a way that inspires visitors of all traditions.

We can start to pray by recapturing these "touchstone" moments. First of all we need to identify them, which we might do by reviewing our lives up to the present. It is easier to do this by thinking of the periods we have spent as infants, at school and college, in different jobs and locations, on vacation and traveling, rather than year by year.

The journal that is included in this pack can help. Use a page for each period and jot thoughts down at random without censoring or sifting them in any way. This is an exercise of the imagination. Let your memory drift back and forth until it fastens on particular moments. These need not be "religious" moments—few of us feel the "right way" at such times! It may take a little while to realize why a particular point in time is revealing itself to you. Just stay with it, making a note in your journal to come back to it later.

It can be helpful to rediscover the effect of such experiences on your different senses or the way your whole body responded to the moment of disclosure. Apply your senses: What did I hear, see, feel, smell at the time? What was it like to be there? Don't force anything. You are just trying to recall some-thing that felt meaningful. Bear in mind that not every memory will be a positive one; for the time being set negative thoughts and sensations aside after making a note of them in the journal.

We call these memories *touchstone experiences* because they provide a standard for considering the rest of our lives. Just as we might recall happy times when we are feeling low, so we can inspire ourselves with our recollections of the sublime when we feel alienated and purposeless. It might also be helpful to think of these experiences as windows into another dimension. It is the experience that matters, not the words with which we try to describe it.

Prayer is an act of memory, but it is not nostalgic or sentimental. We are not trying to restore something that has been lost. In prayer we do not dwell on the past but open ourselves to the future. We are searching all the time for that part of ourselves that is receptive to the outpouring of the holy.

Most of us will soon come to see that touchstone experiences are not of our own making. We were not responsible for what we experienced; rather, it came to us as a gift. The feelings we have when we begin to pray and identify touchstone experiences are of gratitude and humility. We feel small and humbled by what is revealed to us. We are naturally moved to praise and adoration of the divine even if we believe it remains hidden from us. This is why prayer in all the traditions begins with words of glory and thanksgiving. Perhaps you can add words of praise to your journal to mark your progress on the journey of prayer.

Adoration is the most fundamental kind of prayer. It belongs to the very heart of the spiritual life. Because the divine is unique and absolute, it calls forth from us the prayer of adoration. For the deepest feeling that the divine evokes in us, *adoration* is probably a more accurate word than the more traditional *praise,* or *worship*. Those terms suggest a relationship based on power or moral superiority, but we do not adore the divine because we feel humbled before its authority or its overwhelming goodness. We do so because we are overawed by its sheer holiness.

The mystics of all traditions declare the divine to be beyond any words we might find to express our response to the sublime but, because they are driven to speak of their experiences, they do turn to the language of human relationships, and *adore* is the word we use to express our deepest feelings of human love. We cannot say more to a loved one than we adore them.

We like to think of ourselves as sovereign individuals who give respect to those who have earned it or otherwise impressed us. The idea of absolute and

unconditional respect or adoration is virtually unknown to us until we fall in love or become the recipients of the unreserved love of others. Then we can become lost in love, knocked off balance by the sheer power of the force that has grasped us and that we find ourselves giving out. So we have a sense of what it means to be seized by the divine and drawn into its mystery. Maybe because we are free to form relationships with those we choose, without having to conform to religious or social expectations, we are also free to use the personal language of love to describe how we feel when taken out of ourselves by the call of the divine.

When we say we adore another person, we sense that we have no other words to truly express our feelings. Thus can the language of love become the silence of adoration. Ultimately we find the only appropriate response to the holy is to offer ourselves in quiet veneration.

DISCOVERING OURSELVES

IN VICTORIAN times it was usual to issue novels in three volumes. The publishers soon realized that they never had to print as many copies of the third volume as of the first. No matter how gripping the book, there are always going to be far more readers who have read the first few chapters than have ever reached the end!

Sadly, this is probably true of prayer as well. Many feel the need for prayer, sense the call of the divine, and start on the spiritual path only to abandon this most thrilling of adventures.

The trouble is that the most difficult stage of prayer comes just after the beginning. It is almost as if the letter "b" was the hardest letter of the alphabet to learn so we give up trying to learn to read.

The reason for this is simple and natural. We begin to sense the presence of the divine in the world and in our lives and we start to feel small. The slightest glimpse of the holy overwhelms us first with excitement and the desire for more but then with the feeling that we are not worthy to be here. Who am I to stand before the majesty that lies at the heart of the universe? Is this not a place for mystics or saints rather than someone like me who hardly has time for prayer and who even now feels the pressure of all those work or home tasks that have to be completed?

We feel small and then we start feeling bad. How can I be "encountering the divine" when my relationships are in such turmoil, when I am cutting so many corners at work, when I recall how I have been mean or cheated others so many times in the past?

All the great spiritual traditions recognize the sense of unworthiness that comes over the pilgrim just after the start of the pilgrimage. Their message in response is not to be disheartened but to persevere, and they offer stories of how the greatest sages and saints have all gone through this period of doubt and despair. But for us today examples of holiness do not seem enough. What once seemed inspiring now comes across as impossibly idealistic and remote from the realities of modern life. So, how do we proceed?

First of all, we must take our negative thoughts and actions seriously. We cannot say that now that we are becoming spiritual individuals our past mistakes don't matter anymore, but nor should we get so preoccupied with them that we become depressed and pessimistic about making any further progress. We need to look at ourselves calmly and carefully to identify those areas of our lives that are in need of attention and healing. One way to address these needs is to imagine you are talking to someone who you trust absolutely, and to whom you can say anything. Then say it! "This is what I feel guilty about"; "I did this, and I have never been able to forget it. It plays on my mind even today."

It should be said here that this is not an exercise in depth psychology. We are not trying to recover hidden memories or retrospectively revise our understanding of the past. There is no forcing or straining involved anywhere in genuine prayer, and certainly not at this moment when we are dealing with such unhappy material. The point now is just to let those guilty feelings come to mind so that we can deal with them—if not once and for all, at least in a way that allows us to continue in prayer.

Another important way of dealing with past mistakes is to look for ways to make up for them. If it seems possible and appropriate, this may be the time to apologize to an individual we have hurt, to say "I have been troubled by what happened between us all that time ago and I would like to make amends. . ." But, as often as not, we will have to accept that the past is past and though there is nothing we can do that will change things there may be some symbolic act we can perform to put our concern to rest. Making an anonymous gift of money to a charity or volunteering some time to a local care project may help us feel we have made amends. The hard part is allowing ourselves to accept that we have done all that we can and must now put the matter behind us.

It is typical of individuals at this stage of prayer not only to be haunted by their own past behavior, but also to be aware of the hurts that they have themselves received from others.

As the divine draws near to us it is inevitable that we will begin to see every aspect of our life in new ways. When we recognize how neglectful we have been of this most critical dimension of reality, it is natural to feel guilty and to focus on our inadequacies. When we reflect on the damaged character of the world and of human relationships, it is likely that we will also ask how responsible we are for our own flawed behavior. Given our upbringing and circumstances, could we have done otherwise? We might start feeling sorry for ourselves and dwelling upon our own individual wounds.

We should be aware that these memories and feelings are coming to the surface because we are starting to see how our lives are in fact part of a much

greater scheme for the world. These very feelings, which we previously thought of as negative and to be kept out of mind, are in fact clues as to our role in the cosmic order. Now that we are seeing the world afresh in the divine light, we can learn who we really are and not just who we pretend to be, or who we claim to be with our résumés of success and achievement.

As human individuals we are formed through our relationships with others within the structures of the world in which we live. We can only ever be partially in control of our life paths. We can never see more than a glimpse of the complexity of the causes and motivations behind all the events that affect and form us. Left on our own, such thoughts make us feel small and irrelevant, but as our sense of the divine grows so does our appreciation of our essential part in the drama of the universe.

As we move through this second moment of prayer, we begin to see how we will come back to the sense of connection and purpose that we had when we recalled our existing relationship with the divine and our memories of sacred presence in our past. We see that we have been purposely knocked off course so that we can learn how to integrate all the facets of our personality and history in the light of what we have seen. At last, we stand before the holy in the entirety of ourselves, sorry and accepting, and inspired to journey on.

We have also taken a step in understanding ourselves as spiritual beings. We have recognized the importance of *sacred awareness*—the constant examination of our thoughts and feelings in the perspective of the divine experience. Sacred awareness is the great gift we take with us from this moment. From now on we will try to see every aspect of our life in a new way. Daily life is divine life.

The traditions define the responsibilities of humankind as love of the divine and love of our fellow beings. As we become aware of the divine dimension of our life, at the very heart of our being, we quickly realize how we have failed to live in accordance with our true nature.

Growing in prayer and developing spiritually bring this awareness of our shortcomings. It is a sign of our increased sensitivity and progress and should lead not to fear and shame but to a determination to improve ourselves and the distorted structures of society. In short, we are called to "conversion" not from one set of beliefs to another, but to a profound change of heart that involves turning away from negative behavior and turning toward responsible living.

We cannot hope to know immediately how to act in each and every circumstance, but if we are prepared to allow our lives to be orientated toward the divine, we can be confident that we will soon begin to be liberated from the anxiety associated with decision making.

The conscience is often described as the moral meeting place between the individual soul and the sacred. If we act according to our conscience, we will

come to recognize that what is right is also what is best for us. The focus at this stage is on the past. We need to come to terms with who we have been in order to move forward and beyond. The prayer called for here is known as *confession*.

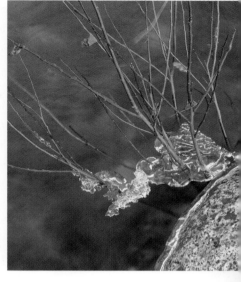

Confession is the acknowledgment of our failure to live and act appropriately. It is the verbal expression of our determination to change. It brings our failings out into the open in order to relieve us of the burden of shame and also the temptation of despair.

Confession is made to or before the divine but it can also be made to other people. Today we believe that serious failings are those that have a damaging effect on other people so, even if we cannot ask forgiveness of the actual "victims," there is a certain consistency in making an admission of fault to someone else. We may be members of a faith community that provides for formal or informal confession, or we might be able to share our memories with another praying person who accepts an agreement of confidentiality and who understands the process in which we are engaged.

In Hasidic Judaism, confession can be made to a spiritual mentor or to a trustworthy friend. All should be revealed, nothing concealed, so that the power of the evil inclination can be destroyed and its hold over the individual broken.

Probably the most important characteristic of the prayer of confession made during our spiritual journey is spontaneity. We are moved to confess by our growing perception of the sacred in our life. After spending some time in the prayer of awareness, we are profoundly aware of the need for conversion and reconciliation. Only through confession can we find reassurance and the freedom of spirit to move into a more active participation in the divine.

DEEPER INTO THE DIVINE

*W*E HAVE encountered the mystery of the divine in our lives and have responded to the challenge the sacred presence brings to our attitudes and actions. We have begun to see ourselves as spiritual beings and are making the effort to live accordingly.

No longer beginners on the spiritual path, we are now adventuresome travelers who are ready to go deeper into the unknown territory where we are convinced we will find the goal of our journey, the experience of the community between human and divine.

A simple Buddhist parable describes the way we are moving. A pilgrim sets out for the sun shining beyond the mountains. Its heat and light draw him on, but as he moves toward it he finds the ascent becoming steeper and the way

rough and paved with jagged rocks and broken pathways. Worse still, the sun is sinking behind the hills. Evening falls. It is cold and dark and the pilgrim begins to question whether the sun was really there at all or if the effort to reach it is worth making. He wonders whether he is really entitled to make the journey and all sorts of thoughts about his past actions come back to haunt him and reinforce his doubts. He lights a few candles for warmth and light and falls asleep, resolved to return home in the morning. But when morning comes the sun is shining again and the candles have burned out. It is warmer and brighter than at the beginning of his journey because he is closer to his goal. His doubts of the previous night have burned out like the candles. So he continues the climb. It is still several days before he reaches the peak, but each night is a little warmer and never quite so dark as the first. It does not matter that he has run out of candles. When he crosses the mountaintop he sees a vast and seemingly endless land spread out before him. There are forests and rivers, hills and valleys, towns and fields. He is filled with the desire to explore this country. Suddenly a wind builds up that propels him down the mountainside and into a forest. The next part of his journey begins here. He has no map, but he has the memory of what he saw briefly from the mountaintop and the sun still shining above the trees.

On our spiritual journey divine reality draws us on, and as we proceed the desire to go further increases. The fear now is that we may become disorientated, not because we are in a new country, but because we are trying to live in the same old world in a completely new way. That is why we must maintain the habit of prayer. The prayer period becomes like the pilgrim's moment on the mountaintop when he perceived all that lay before him. If only he could have remembered the scene photographically, he would have had a map for his journey.

We have an advantage over the pilgrim because we already have some knowledge of the country we are entering. People have made the journey before and left accounts and records of their journeys. Travelers' tales are not guidebooks designed to give exact locations, precise distances, and opening

times. They are personal accounts written long after the journey has been made. They present the story not so much as it happened but more as it *should* have happened. Travel writers tend to be rather eccentric individuals and we can't always be confident that they are telling the truth. Yet, when we read them, and especially if we read accounts by several writers who have explored the same territory, we begin to form an image of the place that will help orient us when we make our own, inevitably very different, journeys.

At this stage of prayer we make use of the scriptures and writings of the traditions to help us go deeper into the sacred nature of the territory we already inhabit. We may have been brought up to think of such writings as supremely authoritative and we may have been told to take their content literally as the only possible way of expressing spiritual truths. We may have reason to doubt such claims, especially as we have come into contact with other traditions that challenge our inherited understanding or give new insights. In short, we have been used to treating sacred texts as guidebooks rather than as travel writings, and so we have come to think of the spiritual journey as a matter of following directions rather than imaginative wandering.

Now our desire and intention is to deepen our relationship with the divine by exploring

some of the various ways in which the sacred has already been communicated to humankind. The prayer of this stage has been called *meditation* or *mental prayer* because it is conducted silently and it is very personal. It involves trying to hear the holy word that is being spoken to us through texts, through nature, and through other people. Its purpose is to make us more aware of how close the divine is to us and how intensely the world is charged with the power of the sacred.

This kind of prayer is likely to be new to most seekers because, unlike praise and confession, it has traditionally been reserved for religious "professionals" like monks and nuns who are able to devote lengthy periods of time to its practice. But the duration of the practice is not as important as its regularity.

Most people will be able to find some time for frequent prayer and for some of the exercises suggested here. Furthermore, we now appreciate more clearly that the spiritual and the everyday cannot be simply distinguished from one another, and those who live and pray in the world may have far more intense experiences of interacting with the divine than those who permanently withdraw.

The prayer of meditation is designed to help us to identify the divine thread that is interwoven in the material of our ordinary lives. The immediate goal is a deepened personal spirituality, but we will discover that that in itself leads us to a more profound sense of our involvement with and responsibility for the world beyond ourselves. So we appreciate once again that prayer is not so much something we do as a dynamic process which, once entered, takes us up and carries us along.

In meditation we use our minds to reflect on a text or experience so that we can come to a fuller understanding of the spiritual truth found there and welcome it into ourselves.

In the traditions, meditation figures most importantly as "holy reading," a method of paying particular attention to a text so that the reader moves beyond the words to an encounter with their author. Holy reading is not a form of literary criticism by which we hope to identify hidden meanings or the obscure intentions of the author. It is a form of prayer in which the texts have been selected not because of their intrinsic merits but because they have been recognized as carrying sacred meaning. They have been accepted as scripture by a community—a reminder that though we may pray alone we do not do so in isolation. Prayer may be an individual activity but it is not an

independent one. As soon as we begin to pray, we join a fellowship of spiritual seekers that cuts across all boundaries of race, gender, and religion.

Holy reading has also been called "praying the scriptures," which emphasizes the fact that there is also an active character to meditation. We do not simply listen; we speak in prayer, entering into dialogue with the author of the text to bring about a genuine conversation through which we can develop a true relationship.

The method of holy reading is quite simple. First, we identify a text to ponder and open it before us. Second, we still our bodies and minds as we enter into the presence of the divine. We then read slowly through the text for five or ten minutes, pausing or restarting as seems right to us. We read as if we were listening to a soft-spoken wise person sharing wisdom with us. Finally, we rest in silence to allow a word or phrase we have read to present itself for us to take away from the exercise with gratitude. Later in our day, and especially before we retire for the night, we briefly recall the divine gift, the presented word or words, noting them down in our prayer journal, perhaps adding a few words of our own in response.

The most practical aspect of holy reading is the relatively short time actually spent reading. In holy reading we do not seek to complete a chapter or section in the prayer time; instead, we set a time limit on our reading. This means that we need not feel pressure to move on but may comfortably pass back and forth through the text. It means also that we can give more attention to the words and phrases themselves without worrying about the style or context of the passage.

Because holy reading is not reading for information, it can provide an opportunity for exploring other traditions; however, it is closer to the spirit of this kind of prayer to use texts from our own faith background or those that we have come across naturally rather than texts chosen deliberately to increase our knowledge of other cultures.

If we are using a book of scriptures for our holy reading, we will come to appreciate through our prayer how these writings were selected for special status. We may then wish to reverence the book in some special way because it is our conduit to the divine.

We will not want to treat it just like any other book but will want to treasure it by keeping it in a special place or on a special stand. In Christian churches the Gospel book is often left open on a lectern with a light burning before it. Muslims place the Qur'an on a small folding wooden stand when reading it prayerfully. In synagogues, the Torah scroll is kept in the sacred ark and the text is not touched with the fingers but followed with a pointer, usually in the form of a human hand. Tibetan Buddhist scriptures are stored wrapped in silk when not being read.

If we are using different sources for our prayerful reading we may not begin with a volume to revere, although as we proceed, the prayer journal in which we record gifted words may come to be a personal scripture that we want to copy out in a fair hand in a finely bound book. Some traditions have rituals for enthroning texts in these personal volumes or consecrating prayer journals.

TRANSFORMING THE WORLD

OR MOST of us, prayer is simply about asking for things: for ourselves, for others, or for some purpose. We believe we cannot achieve something through our own power or abilities so we look beyond for help. It's not surprising that those who are skeptical about religious belief see it as an expression of frustration or desperation, particularly on the part of those who are powerless in society or facing overwhelming difficulties in their personal lives.

For those who have a sense of the divine this prayer of petition or *intercession,* as it is called, raises a moral difficulty. Am I truly entitled to what I am asking for? Are there not a thousand more deserving cases than mine? How will the granting of my request affect others in ways I cannot possibly foresee?

The best way to understand this kind of prayer is to see how it fits into the dynamic of prayerful existence that we have been exploring. Although it appears to be the simplest and most obvious type of prayer, it really belongs to an advanced moment in our spiritual development. This doesn't mean that it is wrong for beginners to offer this kind of prayer, nor that we should feel bad about turning to the divine for help when we are in need even if we have been neglecting our spiritual progress.

We dare to approach the divine with our petitions because we experience the divine as caring, embracing, forgiving, and involved in the world and in our lives. Our intimation of the transcendent dimension of all that is has made us look again at our life and attitudes. This brought us to a sense of acceptance by and oneness with the depths of being. We now come to focus not on ourselves and our failings but on others and their needs. Our first taste of the divine made us turn inward to examine and assess our life, but we persevered and

found that the divine was big enough to deal with our petty shortcomings. Now, as we dwell more deeply in the sacred, we are compelled to look outward to identify the needs of others and of the world which we see afresh as a holy place.

Far from being a despondent kind of prayer, petition rightly understood is a profound expression of our spiritual identity. It points to our solidarity with the divine and reveals the character of the sacred as oriented toward our benefit and salvation. The more we know the divine, the more we strive to improve the world; the more we strive to make the world better, the deeper our spirituality becomes.

There is nothing wrong with praying for ourselves so long as we believe that our requests are consonant with the unfolding of the divine in history. The most we can do is sense this unfolding because we can never see the complete picture of how all actions and events interrelate. But spiritual teachers have suggested that as our relationship with the sacred deepens we can determine whether or not our actions and prayers are in tune with the divine project.

Good deeds produce positive results even in the short term for us to recognize them and realize the appropriateness of our actions. Similarly, bad actions produce negative results. Most of us will have a feeling that what we are doing is right or wrong. We ought to follow our consciences, but we should accept that our consciences need to be informed and educated. This might mean considering the chain of events an act of ours is likely to set in process rather than just thinking about the deed itself.

We need to practice doing good if we are to become good at it. So it is with prayer. A little thought will help us to recognize whether or not what we are asking for is a selfish desire or a genuine good. But prayer is not primarily an intellectual activity so it is to the feelings rather than the thoughts that accompany our petitions that we must pay special attention. How do I feel when I pray? Does prayer make me happy or sad? Is it comforting or disturbing? It isn't so much that "happy" and "comforting" are good while "sad" and "disturbing" are bad; the point is that our feelings are indicators of our spiritual state.

This is perhaps most clearly seen with prayers of personal petition. If they are accompanied by a sense of discomfort or unease, we might conclude that we should subject them to scrutiny. We need to be careful to distinguish the feelings brought about by the prayers from those that led to them in the first place. This is called *discernment*, and is something that will grow in us as our spirituality deepens. In the traditions, discernment is fostered through conversations with a prayer guide or a spiritual companion (see pages 64–67).

It is a good idea to keep a record of the things we ask for ourselves in prayer. This could just be a list in our journal, but many people have found it more helpful to enter the record randomly in single words or very short phrases on a plain page. The reason for this is that what we ask for can tell us more about

ourselves and our concerns and needs. The random entry method, as opposed to the list method, makes it clearer that a personality is being pictured here— our own. We have a responsibility to care for ourselves and we may discover that the answer we receive to our prayers of petition is not the granting of small requests but a new insight into our own identity.

The second type of petition is prayer for others, also called *intercession*. We pray for people who are sick, or in some kind of trouble. It is quite literally the least we can do and sometimes the most when, for example, the individuals are far from us or in need of specialized help or treatment.

Intercession is closely related to prayer for ourselves, but it derives from a deepening of our relationship with the divine. If personal petition is a cry to the divine for help, intercession might be thought of as a reaching out toward others from the divine that we now recognize and experience within our own being. It is because we have come closer to the sacred that we are propelled away from ourselves in a concerned movement toward others. Saint Basil, an early Christian writer, asked: "How can we love God if we cannot love our fellow human beings?"

We pray for others because we have discovered something new about the nature of the divine. The transcendent ground of all reality and being is not a passive foundation or principle, but an active and living heart. No wonder that the heart is used so much in religious imagery.

As we discover the divine as the heart of the universe so we come to see more clearly the interrelatedness of all that is and how our prayer moves naturally from an expression of concern for people to a desire to promote the well-being of the natural world.

Modern science is sometimes portrayed as antagonistic toward or even undermining of religious belief, but it has certainly made us more conscious of the interconnections between all that exists and the way that the human, animal, vegetable, and natural realms interact. Today we are aware of ourselves as part of the environment rather than as beings set apart from it or even over it. In fact, it is probably true to say that of all beings we are probably the most reliant on others. Our claim to dominion over nature reveals itself as an expression of our substantial dependence upon it.

The third prayer of petition we find ourselves roused toward is the expression of our yearning for the well-being of the environment. This third kind of prayer, which can be called *active* or *dynamic prayer*, also moves outward, but it more clearly raises the question of our cooperation with the divine in the maintenance of the material world. In short, we realize that prayer needs to be accompanied by action.

The deeper our prayer the more we come to glimpse the nature of the divine as an active and sustaining force in our lives and in the world, and so the more confident we are in calling upon the divine in our time of need. But the more we see that the divine is constantly active in the world, that we are relating to a movement rather than an axiom, the more we are impelled to participate in the ongoing creative activity.

The Western traditions have perhaps overemphasized the picture of creation as an event at the beginning of history, something completed and now usually seen as being in decline and in need of restoration. The result has been that individuals immediately think of themselves as failures caught up in and to a degree responsible for the degeneration from the original perfect state of affairs. All they can do in a world that is itself diseased is cry out for help or take minor defensive measures against further deterioration.

The Eastern traditions, through the idea of *karma,* have more clearly stressed the connection between individual actions and their consequences in the world, but they have represented the world as an illusion and something to be escaped from rather than as a continuous expression of the divine. If Western traditions, through the doctrine of creation, have turned the divine into a god of judgment, the Eastern, through doctrines of karma and rebirth, have removed the divine from the world into an eternal realm to which we hope to escape.

Praying in petition is the simplest kind of prayer. It is what most people understand by the word *prayer*. But this simplest kind of prayer has revealed to us a secret: we dare to ask because we have already received. Prayer is the

language of the divine and we discover we can already speak it. We can speak it because we are related to the divine, and the more we speak it the more fluent we become. Through the language of prayer our relationship with the divine becomes deeper, and as we become more intimate we are inspired to live the divine life in the world. We can speak to the divine in prayer in any human language, without any words at all, but perhaps do so most appropriately through active commitment to the divine plan for the world. The secret that we have received is that prayer is not something we do in daily life, it *is* daily life lived in active communion with the divine.

BECOMING HOLY

*A*S WE progress in prayer we will come to know ourselves more closely than ever before. As we become intimate with the divine we come to rest in that relationship at a point of balance. Think of human love, how it can move from passion through friendship to a kind of communion that couples who have spent years together seem to share and that needs no expression in words. Our relationship with the eternal is timeless, so we will find ourselves at rest with the divine in different ways at various times in our lives.

If we have followed the spiritual path in our lives it is natural that as we grow older many of us will find ourselves settling into a more contemplative kind of prayer. For some, the contemplative (often portrayed as the goal of prayer) will have been an experience of our middle years—rarely of our youth—to which we return in the days of repose.

In contemplation we are not so much praying about or for someone or something as simply experiencing and enjoying the presence of the divine in our hearts and lives.

At the beginning of our spiritual journey we glimpsed and identified traces of the divine in our lives, touchstone experiences that inspired us and called out to us to recognize and explore our true spiritual nature. We realized that our cry for help in times of personal distress or when confronted with injustice or misfortune in the world was not merely an expression of frustration but actually a kind of memory of a power that could heal, forgive, and transform. Our positive and negative feelings and experiences both pointed to the reality of the divine ground of existence and of the personal character of the sacred. We came to see how different kinds of prayer derived from and depended on

this memory of the sacred and so we set aside time to intensify the sense of ourselves as spiritual beings. This journey made us consider our relationships with ourselves, with other people, and with the world. It naturally led us into different kinds of prayer as we came to discover our point of balance, our sense of harmony with the universe.

At the last stage or moment of prayer we find ourselves once more with our sense of the sacred. We have returned to the beginning, but are now armed with the wisdom that comes from experience. We find ourselves drawn in rather than pushed out. We are entitled to enjoy the sacred because we have responded to the divine call to change ourselves and to care for others and the world. This harmony, this drawing in, this enjoyment is what is meant by the prayer of contemplation.

In English usage contemplation has become slightly confused with meditation. Meditation is best thought of as an activity of the mind. The word originally meant study or practice. In the Christian tradition it was sometimes called *mental prayer* because it involved systematic reflection on a religious idea or image. Contemplation, on the other hand, derives from the idea of looking beyond words and images into the very nature of things. This kind of looking involves not just the mind but the whole being, and so contemplation has often been described as an activity of the heart. Another way of putting this is to say that in meditation there is still an "I" that is looking and an object that is being looked at, whereas in contemplation where there is no such distinction; awareness is direct and immediate.

In this life, except perhaps for the very few, such direct perception of the divine can be hoped for only occasionally and will be experienced as a gift rather than as the result of our efforts in prayer.

Through meditation we can prepare ourselves to receive that gift or to recognize it when it comes. We cannot say when we are going to fall in love or make someone fall in love with us. But neither will happen unless we make ourselves available to other people and reach out to them in a spirit of friendship and generosity.

There are traditionally two ways of understanding contemplation which reflect the two basic human personality types identified by the psychologist C.G. Jung: the extrovert and the introvert. Some people are more stimulated and inspired by the outer world, others more by the inner world. This is not to say that some people are spiritual and some are not, for everyone is by nature a spiritual being, but rather that the two types represent two fundamental ways of speaking about and journeying into the divine.

These two kinds of contemplation have been called the positive way and the negative way, or the way of affirmation and the way of denial.

The positive way is a way of describing the divine that emphasizes the similarity between the sacred realm and the ordinary world. The divine may be spoken of using concepts such as motherhood, fatherhood, truth, love, and so on, but always with the qualification that these words cannot do justice to the perfection of the sacred. We use them in order to leave them behind.

The positive way is the path of praise, adoration, and thanksgiving in which we hope through words to rise above language to a pure vision of the holy.

The negative way stresses that no words can adequately express the nature of the divine and so it is better to abandon the attempt and "enter the darkness" by rejecting all thoughts and words and lifting up the heart in love to the holy unknown. Hindus speak of the divine as "not-this; not that," Buddhists of the "void" of truth, and in Zen paradoxical statements called *koans* are meditated on to try to break the link between human language and divine reality.

Extroverts are supposed to be in the majority and so "successful" religious traditions tend to be those that offer opportunities for music, dance, and group activity. Introverts prefer the silence, space, and atmosphere that facilitate quiet reflection. But just as no one is completely of one "type," so at times in our prayer lives we might find ourselves drawn one way, at other times to the other. It is important not to exclude the other way just because it does not seem to appeal to us personally; it is also vital not to confuse the route with the destination by becoming tied to either the words or the silence.

Followers of both paths risk the charge of elitism: the positive by seeming to require an exaggerated visible enthusiasm in prayer and praise; the negative by apparently demanding a posture of asceticism and a mystical detachment from the world. The reality is that holiness is the objective of life for all and therefore must be attainable by all according to their character and experience.

In this final moment we return to the beginning and our intimations of the divine secret of all existence. The glimpses of the sacred that we detected in our lives and in the world when we started to pray have become part of our ordinary vision of life. Increasingly we read the world as a sacred text with ourselves as characters in it. But we need to put the text aside, as a child learning to swim needs to abandon the buoyancy aid and trust itself to the water.

The fourteenth-century English mystic who wrote *The Cloud of Unknowing* says we need to put between ourselves and our words and thoughts, both worldly and spiritual, a "cloud of forgetting." We need to "un-know" all we have learned so nothing remains between us and our contemplation of the divine.

PART TWO

THE WAY OF PRAYER

CREATING A PRAYER SPACE

OUR ABILITY to communicate with the divine is a precious gift. Although we sense that our whole lives are built on the foundation of the holy and that our aim is constant communion with the divine, to begin with we struggle to find the space, the time, and the words with which to come into the presence of the sacred. Jesus said: "When you pray, enter into a private place, shut the door, and pray to your Father who is in secret."

Few of us will have a whole room to set aside as a private chapel or shrine, although sometimes there is an alcove or a space under the stairs which can accommodate a chair or cushion and become our prayer space.

Christians in the Western traditions have marked a place for prayer with a crucifix or cross on the wall or with a prayer desk or *prie-dieu* with a cushion for kneeling and a desk for the Bible or prayer book.

Eastern Christians have an icon corner in their main room where a holy picture is placed, often with a hanging lamp burning before it and in the direction of which family and individual prayers are spoken. A shelf may be reserved for sacred books and images, often just postcards or tear-sheets, along with devotional items such as palm crosses and small incense burners.

An altar was originally a place for sacrifice, but in most traditions it has come to mean the central and most sacred place in a church or temple or the focus of devotion in a private house.

In Hinduism and Buddhism the domestic altar or shrine is a typical feature in homes of the devout. It usually consists of an image of the Buddha or of one or more divinities with provision for flowers, lamps, incense, and food offerings as well as the less formal items that are naturally placed here, such as photographs of teachers and mementoes of pilgrimages.

The modern Western seeker, having identified a place for personal prayer, will almost certainly wish to decorate it with objects of devotion. These may be drawn from the great traditions or from personal experience of the divine. It's best to avoid too much clutter as well as clashing images from different cultures, but anything that is helpful is appropriate.

The domestic shrine is the place to keep sacred texts, the scriptures of the traditions, or an anthology you have collected yourself. Your personal prayer journal may also be kept here. Books of this kind are often wrapped in a piece of silk or other attractive material.

Religious practitioners nearly always acknowledge the sacred character of a shrine or altar by bowing or prostrating before it at the beginning and end of prayer or worship. Such practices may seem somewhat forced to the contemporary seeker, but an act of marking off time when coming to this sacred place can help deepen prayer time. A candle may be lit on arrival and extinguished on departing, a stone moved, or a picture or book uncovered— whatever distinguishes the prayer time from a casual passing through the space.

Although we have suggested moving to a special place for prayer we should remember that prayer is not an escapist activity but should return us to the world invigorated by the spirit and determined to transform what we find

there. One way of doing this is to bring to our altar items that relate to our concerns in prayer such as pictures of those for whom we would like to pray.

Similarly, we may choose a position that expresses the mood of our prayer. Generally we will select a comfortable position, such as sitting on a chair, hands placed on our knees, or cross-legged on a cushion, or on a low prayer stool.

FINDING THE TIME FOR PRAYER

*L*ACK OF time is the great complaint many of us make today. Finding time for prayer means cramming more activity into an already busy day and almost certainly neglecting some other vital part of our responsibilities. Yet if prayer is so essential to our well-being, how can it really be so hard to fit in?

The mistake most of us make is thinking that prayer requires a lot of time, or rather that it requires a lot of time all at once. Instead, think of prayer as a language. If we want to learn a new language we can start by learning just one word a day. But we rarely do that. We try to learn long lists of words all at once. The lists are usually constructed thematically but without relevance to our present concerns and activity. We have all laughed at those old-fashioned phrase books with a sentence for every kind of unlikely eventuality that might confront us on our journey to some remote and exotic destination: "Tether my camel while I inquire about engaging a servant." How many words do we need to communicate simply but clearly? How many words do we actually use regularly in our native language? A few hundred, perhaps? One word a day and we will soon be well on our way.

There is a type of prayer that involves only one or two words at a time. It is called *ejaculatory prayer*. The essence of each of the moments of prayer we have been considering can be concentrated and expressed in a single word: Praise! Forgive! Reveal! Care! Transform! In Hinduism the sacred mantra *Om* expresses all that there is to be said about the meaning and purpose of life. The early Christians often prayed with the single word *Abba*. This means "father" in the Aramaic language that Jesus himself spoke and so sums up the relationship with God. The constant prayer of Muslims is *Allahu Akbar* ("God is great").

Such short prayers have the intensity of exclamations like Fire! or Help! or even Wow! They concentrate all we want to say or can say in one syllable. The hearer knows exactly what these words mean and responds appropriately. Short prayers are profound prayers because they remind us that, in the end, prayer is beyond words, both in the sense that the divine does not need to be told our thoughts and in the sense that no words can express the majesty of the sacred. Short prayers help us to realize that prayer is easy and comes naturally to us.

Rituals can also help us to make time for prayer. The performance of short and simple ceremonies such as lighting a candle, unveiling an image, or placing a flower before a picture focuses the mind and engages the body for a moment or so in prayer.

Once we realize how easy it is to find time for prayer, we can identify suitable times for prayer. Muslims are required to pray five times a day—at dawn,

noon, afternoon, sunset, and evening. Christian monks traditionally pray "the hours" seven times a day. The timing of these prayers reflects the natural rhythm of the day. Most of us would agree that important times for prayer would be first thing in the morning in preparation for all that is to come during our waking hours and last thing at night when we review the day so we can sleep comfortably and resolve to act differently if need be the following day.

By getting into the habit of praying at particular times—for however short a period—we begin to recognize ourselves as pilgrims embarked on a spiritual journey. We know when and where our next formal engagement with the divine is to take place and this gives us a sense that the day is consecrated to the sacred and not just a period of time to be endured.

Some people find that limiting prayer to the extremes of the day initially brings a stronger sense of desiring to pray at some other time in between. It is as though by trying to confine the divine that we find it bursting out elsewhere. When we feel ready we should try to find a time, preferably daily, when we can come into the presence of the sacred in a more personal way, a time that is our own rather than the sun's or the moon's.

Our personal prayer period is the time when we practice or exercise spiritually. It is when we explore the mystery that is the heart of the world. It is best to endeavor to establish a prayer period that lasts for a fixed length of time and takes place in the same location each day. This is not because the divine is under our control, but because this regularity can help us to discern the subtle movements that take place within us as we grow spiritually.

It's hard to do nothing for long. Just try sitting still for five minutes without any distractions such as music or a view. Of course praying isn't doing nothing, but it does mean we have to be with ourselves in a way that we may not be used to, without other activities to keep our mind off this challenging encounter. Establish how long you can sit still and then make that the length of your prayer period to begin with. Better still, add just a minute or two—because you are not alone.

BEGINNING TO PRAY

*H*AVING identified a place, a time, and a duration for prayer, you are ready to begin the journey of a lifetime. Give thanks that you are able to do this and remind yourself that, however new or strange the adventure seems, you are doing something completely natural, something without which your life is incomplete. You are becoming the spiritual being you have always been but have not allowed yourself to recognize.

A good way to begin is by *centering*. You need to turn your attention from the outside world and its distractions to your inner being, your point of contact with the divine. Centering is a form of preparation for prayer rather than prayer itself. It is valuable both at the beginning of your spiritual journey and also, briefly, at the start of any prayer period to help you move within.

One way to begin centering is by paying attention to the sounds surrounding you as you sit in your prayer place. We live in a noisy world and wherever you are there is unlikely to be complete silence. Try to be aware of all the different sounds you can hear, then see if you can separate each from the other. Simply stay with the sounds. There is no need to identify the particular species of bird whose song you can hear! Just allow the sounds to surround you, accepting that they are outside of you and pose no threat to your intention of moving within. Then let the sounds go. Allow them to fade into the background. Try to become aware of your own presence before the divine.

When you come to your prayer period it is best to arrive prepared. You don't want to use the time trying to think of something to do.

Spiritual Direction—The Journey

IN THE great traditions those who are seriously committed to prayer are encouraged to seek out a spiritual director or guide, a "guru" or "soul friend," who can advise them on the content of prayer. Such an individual needs to have insight into the progress we are making on our spiritual journey. Spiritual direction calls for a particular aptitude as well as experience and training. Spiritual directors or guides need to have experienced prayer if they are to be our companions on the way. Spiritual companionship is not an academic qualification that can be achieved; it is a gift that certain praying individuals receive, which brings them into conversation with others on the path. The sign of a genuine soul friend is willingness to learn from their fellow travelers.

Finding a spiritual guide needs to be handled very carefully, particularly by those outside of any religious affiliation. If you feel the need for a guide, it is best to make it your prayer that someone will be revealed to you, rather than turning immediately to the classified ads. By participating in organized religious activity, even on the fringes, you will sometimes come across individuals who, rather than putting themselves forward, are recommended by their reputations. Always remember that you are not looking for someone to tell you what to do, but someone who is capable of listening to you and bringing their own experience into the dialogue.

If the relationship doesn't work out, don't allow yourself to be trapped in it. There is no need to enter into a contract as you might with a therapist or counselor. Every meeting should end with you being in charge of deciding whether or not to return.

You may be aware of a friend or acquaintance who is also trying to pray. Getting together to exchange experiences and ideas is likely to be helpful to both of you. It shouldn't really matter if one is more advanced than the other. Growing in prayer is not like physical growth where you keep on going until you stop. It is more cyclical, a moving forward and a return before moving forward again. The more you grow in prayer, the more you become aware of any incompleteness that you need to return to. Spiritual growth is more dynamic than physical growth because you can always go back and do things differently and there will never come a time when it is too late to start again.

Coming together with others on the journey of prayer will help us to see how each spiritual journey is unique, even if the route and destination are identical, as the following story shows:

Four men traveled along the same route during different seasons. One struggled along featureless snow-covered tracks; another along pretty lanes with green borders; a third remembered roads busy with people on vacation admiring the blooming flowers; the fourth had hurried along broken trails as the wind brought the leaves from the trees and the sky began to darken.

Although each one arrived safely at their destination, none knew the route well enough to guide and advise future travelers. They would need to make the journey again and again to be fully aware of what might be encountered. No individual is the director or guide any more than another. Even one who has just started out on the journey will have traveler's tales to tell.

If we find ourselves praying alone with neither contact nor knowledge of other pilgrims, we might be able to make use of the "inner guide." To pray is to enter into a relationship with the divine and so we can never really say we are praying alone. As soon as we speak the divine is listening and moving toward a response. In the traditions it is usually said that we speak in prayer because we have already been spoken to. It is actually our prayer that is the response to the divine movement toward us. However hesitant, unformed, or inarticulate our prayer, it is not words being poured out into a void, but an attempt to reply to the power addressing us.

Prayer is a response to the one who is encouraging us to speak, leading us in the direction in which we must go. What better guide can we have than the divine itself? The trouble is that the sacred voice must be heard through the cacophony of other voices calling out for our attention. The Bible calls the voice of God a "still, small voice," but rather than straining our ears to hear this voice it is better to identify the distinctive way in which it speaks. Writers on prayer refer to a "spiritual sense" that we all share and whereby we can detect the clues of sacred communication.

DETACHED CURIOSITY

*T*HE divine speaks to us, it has been said, directly but in an indirect way. Our everyday lives are full of messages from the divine, but we need to learn how to read them. Essentially what we need to do is to become more aware, more conscious of what is around us. We need to develop an attitude of detached curiosity toward the outside world.

Detached curiosity means noticing what you notice and trying to understand why. On getting home from work or study, or on completing the day's tasks at early evening when the light is beginning to fail, pause for a moment and allow the experiences of the day to run through your mind. The point is to recall the things that registered in your consciousness for no apparent reason: odd and

unusual things, ordinary and commonplace things—the name above a store, the decoration of a window, the expression on someone's face, a snatch of conversation heard in passing. Jot down a word or so in your prayer journal to help you to remember these things and the way they made you feel.

This may seem to be a waste of time at first, but after a while patterns and links start to emerge between these sightings that reveal a deeper meaning. It's like *déjà vu* in reverse. Instead of feeling that we have been in this place before but cannot say when, we are conscious of how a place we seem to know has been constructed from disconnected elements we registered with our detached curiosity. We go to a job interview. We seem to recognize a building or office we have never been in. That's auspicious! But we feel uneasy here even though the prospects of getting the job look good. We recall that the components of this place are all in our journal and that each one was associated with a negative thought. The inner guide is telling us something here.

Detached curiosity pays particular attention to coincidences—when we are made especially aware of the connection between two experiences without having to wait until we spot it through our journaling. It's as if the inner voice is saying, "Watch out!" or "How about this?" We will still need to work on and pray about the message, but we can be certain that something important is being brought to our attention.

The psychologist C.G. Jung used the term *synchronicity* to refer to phenomena that seem to be linked only by chance or coincidence but are meaningfully related to one another and in which people detect a purposeful trend.

Dreams can also deliver clues from the inner guide and Jung has provided a complete vocabulary for understanding and interpreting them. The main significance of dreams is that they mix up all the elements of our personality—memories, hopes, fears, and experiences—and then represent them to us in a new way which has no regard for the realities of time and place. The dream, in other words, does the work of detached curiosity for us. We do not need to try to see things from another angle; here they are all given to us in just that way.

In prayer we need not analyze our dreams, because getting to know ourselves inside out is not our immediate task, but rather see them as resources for prayer, providing material to be prayed over before we move on. As with images that return from the day, dreams should be noted and reviewed occasionally to see what suggestions are being brought to our conscious mind by their content. The recurring character of a dream image may suggest the need to work through it in prayer.

USING THE PRAYER PACK

PRAYER JOURNAL

The 64-page journal included with this pack will become your private, personal account of your prayer life. You can use it to record touchstone moments that inspire you to pray and to make a note of prayers that are meaningful to you. You can paste in pictures that you find inspiring or that have spiritual significance for you and will assist in entering a state of prayerful meditation or contemplation. Turning the pages of your journal and spending a few moments on each image can be a helpful form of prayer. If you are praying for loved ones, it is natural to do so with their pictures in front of you. You may keep photographs of your loved ones in the journal so that they are on hand at your prayer times.

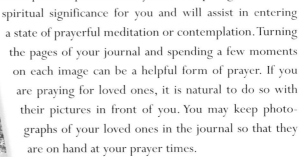

As you pray, images or words may come into your mind—note these in your journal as soon as you have finished praying. You will probably see a pattern emerging over a period of time that will focus your prayer on areas of your life that may need attention. You can also make a note of how you have spent your prayer time each day: for whom and for what intentions you have prayed; what feelings, thoughts, and images came to you. These insights will become the touchtones of tomorrow.

When you read from the scriptures or engage in any other form of "holy reading," words or phrases may stay with you long after you have finished

O LORD, ANSWER US IN
THE DAY OF TROUBLE.
SEND US HELP FROM YOUR
HOLY PLACE.
SHOW US THE PATH OF LIFE,
FOR IN YOUR PRESENCE IS JOY.
GIVE JUSTICE TO THE ORPHAN
AND OPPRESSED
AND BREAK THE POWER OF
WICKEDNESS AND EVIL.
LOOK UPON THE HUNGRY
AND SORROWFUL
AND GRANT THEM THE HELP
FOR WHICH THEY LONG.
LET THE HEAVENS REJOICE AND
THE EAR BE GLAD;
MAY YOUR GLORY ENDURE
FOREVER.

(from the Judeo-Christian tradition)
The European Province of the Society of Saint Francis 1992

reading. Make a note of these in your journal as they will be of significance to you in your prayer life.

You will find that not only does your journal provide a record of how you spend your prayer time, but will also aid reflection and meditation and be a source of growing self-awareness and spirituality.

PRAYER CARDS

The twenty prayer cards included in the pack offer an inspiring image that can be used in contemplative prayer on one side and a type of prayer from a range of traditions on the other side. The types of prayer included are: Praise, Confession, Petition, Intercession, Thanksgiving, and Ejaculatory.

Further details of the first five types can be found in Part Three; see pages 58–60 for more information on Ejaculatory prayers. At the beginning of your prayer practice, you may take one of the cards and meditate on the image for several minutes. Then turn the card over and read the prayer several times, contemplating its message and its significance in your life.

CANDLE AND CANDLE HOLDER

Many religious and spiritual traditions use candles during their prayer rituals. The lighting of a candle brings ceremony to prayer and its flame, representing the divine spirit, brings metaphorical as well as actual light.

Prayer Practice

RAYING is a very individual experience, but the following steps may help you to develop your own prayer practices.

Step 1

Prayer should always begin with an act of reverence. Showing respect may take the form of an action such as lighting a candle before an image or speaking a short phrase such as the Buddhist "I take my refuge in the Buddha" or the Muslim *"Bismillah al-Rahman al-Rahim"* ("In the name of Allah, the Compassionate, the Merciful").

Step 2

Next should follow a brief calling to memory and offering in prayer of our intention. This may be simply to go deeper into prayer, or to confess some fault, or to offer intercession for another. Having an intention is one of the ways in which prayer differs from meditation. It reminds us that prayer is by nature a form of communication, not just relaxation.

Step 3

Whatever form the prayer of the day takes, it never involves a syllabus. If during prayer a particular word or feeling strikes you, gently stay with it until the time feels right to move on. If the feeling is a negative one, do not feel obliged to remain there too long. Mark the obstacle mentally and resolve to deal with it later.

STEP 4

As you come toward the end of your prayer period, pause again to focus on your prayer and see if any issue or image is standing out. Enter into conversation with the divine as you might speak to a close friend you can say anything to. Some people find it helpful to picture the divine in a form they feel comfortable chatting with. For traditional adherents this could be Jesus, Krishna, or another saint or prophet; others might prefer a wise woman or holy man. End the conversation with an expression of thanks and affirmation.

STEP 5

End the prayer period with another symbolic action, such as extinguishing the candle, speaking another set of words, or repeating of the first. The words "Thy will be done" from the Christian tradition or "I take my refuge in the *Dharma* (or teaching)" from the Buddhist tradition are appropriate words to end with.

STEP 6

Immediately on completing a prayer period, make a note in your journal of how you used the time and what happened during it—the thoughts, feelings, images, and ideas that occurred to you. There is no need to be systematic about this review. Just fill a page with words.

STEP 7

Before the next prayer period, go back to your journal and look at the last few reviews you have made. Some people set aside a specific time to do this. More than likely, this exercise will provide material for the next period.

PART THREE

Forms of Prayer

INTRODUCTION

*W*hy do people give up praying? Why, having caught a glimpse of the divine, would anyone turn the other way? Why, having tasted the food of life, would you return to the bland fare of ordinary existence?

In this pack I have tried to present prayer as an exciting adventure to which all of us are invited. The problem for most of us in the West is that we tend to confuse prayer in all its fullness with particular forms of it.

It is as if we are learning a new language and have learned only a few verb forms or noun endings. Although we know that the new language will open up a whole new world of culture and communication, we have sacrificed that enrichment because the first few stages are a bit tedious. A journey of a thousand miles begins with a single step, but that first one always seems the hardest.

So with prayer. It is difficult to start. Moreover, because we confuse the beginning of prayer with prayer itself, it may be difficult to continue. Prayer is more than asking God for things or crying out to Him when we are troubled. Prayer has a dynamic, a movement. We need a sense of the journey and an openness to the destination if we are to be true travelers on the spiritual road.

Now we look again at the forms that prayer takes and how they relate to each other. Read through the whole section a couple of times at the beginning of your journey. Return to it during your journey. Constantly remind yourself what prayer is and why it is so important to you. Give thanks for those who have traveled the way before you and enjoy their descriptions of the road. Think of those who will come after you and of the advice you would give them. Remember how far you have already traveled and look to the exciting journey ahead.

PRAISE

OFFER PRAISE because everything that you are and have comes ultimately from the divine. At the beginning of your existence you had the promise of life. At the end you have the hope of eternity. These two are all that matter. Everything else is a gift for the short time that is your life on earth. What will we make of our gifts? Will we be grateful or dissatisfied, envious of others or content with our lot? Will we share what we have?

Praise is how we give thanks for all the riches we experience in our lives and relationships, but as we move deeper into prayer we come to praise the divine for simply being divine. Think of how you honor those who have done nothing

for you directly, but whose contribution to the world is so self-evident that your respect is unquestioned. The more you see the world as the manifestation of the sacred, the more you will wish to esteem the driving force behind it; the more your way of living is one of praise, the greater will be your happiness.

True prayer always begins and ends with praise. Before you bring forward your needs or the needs and concerns of those around you, before you try to pick up your sacred journey and deepen your sense of spiritual selfhood, picture yourself as a newborn baby and then at the end of your life. Who are you, what have you other than what you have been given?

No words can adequately express what you owe to the divine, so always try to express your praise in acts of love and of care toward others and the world.

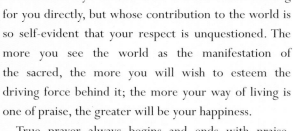

I will exalt you, O God my King,
and bless your name for ever and ever.

Every day will I bless you
and praise your name for ever and ever.

Great is the Lord and highly to be praised;
his greatness is beyond all searching out.

One generation shall praise your works to another
and declare your mighty acts.

They shall speak of the majesty of your glory,
and I will tell of all your wonderful deeds.

They shall speak of the might of your marvelous acts,
and I will also tell of your greatness.

They shall pour forth the story of your abundant kindness
and joyfully sing of your righteousness.

The Lord is gracious and merciful,
long-suffering and of great goodness.

The Lord is loving to everyone
and his mercy is over all his creatures.

All your works praise you, O Lord,
and your faithful servants bless you.

They tell of the glory of your kingdom
and speak of your mighty power,

To make known to all peoples your mighty acts
and the glorious splendor of your kingdom.

PSALM 145: 1–12 (*FROM THE JUDEO-CHRISTIAN TRADITION*)
COMMON WORSHIP, THE ARCHBISHOPS' COUNCIL, 2000

Praise be to you, my Lord, and to all your creation,
especially Brother Sun,
who is our day, and you give us light through him.
And he is beautiful, and shines with great splendor.
From you, Most High, he takes his meaning.

Praise be to you, my Lord,
from Sister Moon and the stars;
in the heavens you have formed them,
shining and precious and beautiful.

Praise be to you, my Lord, from Brother Wind,
and from air and cloud and calm and all weathers
through which you give your creatures nourishment.

Praise be to you, my Lord, from Sister Water
who is so useful and humble and precious and chaste.

Praise be to you, my Lord, from Brother Fire,
through whom you lighten our night:
And he is handsome and merry and vigorous and strong.

Praise be to you, my Lord, from our Sister Mother Earth,
Who nourishes and sustains us,
And brings forth her various fruits,
With many-colored flowers and grasses

ST. FRANCIS OF ASSISI, FROM *"THE CANTICLE OF THE SUN"*
(FROM THE JUDEO-CHRISTIAN TRADITION)
THE EUROPEAN PROVINCE OF THE SOCIETY OF SAINT FRANCIS, 1992

The light which is you shines in all that has life; each spirit is merged
in that light. You are the true one, our joy is to praise you,
and he who adores you finds peace evermore. Trusty and faithful,
all-powerful creator, all of our wants and our needs supply.

(FROM THE SIKH TRADITION)

You are supreme, the infinite spirit,
the highest abode, sublime purifier,
man's spirit, eternal, divine,
the primordial god, unborn, omnipotent.

I bow in homage
before you and behind you;
I bow everywhere
to your omnipresence!
You have boundless strength
and limitless force;
you fulfill
all that you are.

(FROM THE HINDU TRADITION)
THE BHAGAVAD GITA 12, 40 (NEW YORK, BANTAM BOOKS, 1986)

CONFESSION

ACCEPT THAT what you were and are falls short of what you might have been. Coming into contact with the sacred is bound to make you feel uneasy about the way you have lived, and even to make you feel guilty and ashamed about what you have done and the way you have treated other people. But encountering the divine is not like being caught out; it is an experience of liberation and hope. Recognizing that you have been less than perfect inspires you to change for the future and allows you to see that you are not condemned to be a slave of the past.

We have a tendency to dwell on our mistakes, to run through them over and over in our minds, to wish that things had been different. We feel trapped by our past and doubtful of our ability to change. The thought of bringing it all into the open and facing it frightens us, yet it is only by

doing so that we can really deal with the past and move on.

Living with the sacred means receiving the power that can transform all things. The images from the past that haunt you can be emptied of strength if you only open your memory to the divine. On your own you can only relive your memories in pain and shame, but through prayer you can exorcise them of their power to cause you continuing grief.

You should always try to make up for what you have done wrong, but prayer will show you how you can be freed of the most damaging of offenses—those you can do nothing about. Stand before the divine judge and admit your faults and make your promise to be different in the future. Then act accordingly. You are a new creation; live in a way that will express this truth. You have a new life; live every moment with an eye on your autobiography.

Almighty God,
long-suffering and of great goodness:
I confess to you,
I confess with my whole heart
my neglect and forgetfulness of your commandments,
my wrong doing, thinking, and speaking;
the hurts I have done to others,
and the good I have left undone.
O God, forgive me, for I have sinned against you;
and raise me to newness of life . . .

(*FROM THE CHRISTIAN TRADITION*)
COMMON WORSHIP, THE ARCHBISHOPS' COUNCIL, 2000

Seek pardon of the Lord.
He is ever forgiving.
He will let loose the sky for you
in plenteous rain . . .
He will assign unto you gardens and
will give to you rivers.

THE QUR'AN 71.10–14
(*FROM THE MUSLIM TRADITION*)

With my body, speech and mind, humbly I prostrate,
And make offerings both set out and imagined.
I confess my wrong deeds from all time,
And rejoice in the virtues of all.
Please stay until this life of suffering is over,
And teach us the way of liberation.
I dedicate all virtues to great enlightenment.

(FROM THE BUDDHIST TRADITION; ADAPTED)
GESHE KELSANG GYATSO AND MANJUSHRI CENTER, 1990/1996

PETITION

*T*HE LIFE of prayer has a natural movement. At first you sense the reality of the divine in the universe and then more and more as a presence within your own being. To begin with, it feels like you and God, but this moment of praise and joy gives way to darker thoughts of your own distance from the sacred realm. Perseverance reveals the truth of divine forgiveness and personal transformation as you honestly expose your sense of unworthiness and sincerely ask to be different in the future. There comes a moment when you need to give serious thought to your way of life. Is it in accord with your desire to follow the spiritual path? Is your lifestyle one that hinders or stimulates your wish to bring the divine into the world?

Petition may be the prayer of asking about yourself. Who am I? What do I want out of my life? As a praying person you have already given the principal answer to these questions. I am a child of the divine, an agent of the sacred in the world, and I wish to further the coming together of all that will manifest the holy in the world. The big question answered, you will ask yourself a thousand times: What do I do now?

Petition is not just asking *for;* it is asking *about*. It comes to the fore when we are still inexperienced in spiritual matters and need to ponder our choices carefully. Prayer of petition therefore begins with a request for guidance. Before we can ask, we need to know that what we are asking for is right; that is, does it serve our fundamental intention of bringing the world to the holy, and the holy into the world? Only occasionally does the divine explode into the world; more typically we find ourselves gently nudged in a particular direction or drawn to a specific way of life. Pray that you will recognize the clues that dot your path through life.

1 O Lord, I call to you; come to me quickly;
hear my voice when I cry to you.

2 Let my prayer rise before you as incense,
the lifting up of my hands as the evening sacrifice.

3 Set a watch before my mouth, O Lord,
and guard the door of my lips;

4 Let not my heart incline to any evil thing.

PSALM 141: 1–4 (*FROM THE JUDEO-CHRISTIAN TRADITION*)
COMMON WORSHIP, THE ARCHBISHOPS' COUNCIL, 2000

You are all mercy,
Think of me.
You are the enlightened one,
Think of me.
You are the supreme teacher, think of me.

If you do not listen, who will listen?
If you do not give me blessing, who will bless me?
If you do not protect me, who will protect me?
If you do not guide me, who will guide me?

(FROM THE BUDDHIST TRADITION)

All praise be to God,
the Lord of the Universe,
the Most Merciful, the Most Kind,
Master of the Day of Judgment.
You alone do we worship,
From you alone do we seek help.
Show us the straight way.
The way of those you favor,
those who do not anger you
or follow the wrong path.

THE QUR'AN 1
(FROM THE MUSLIM TRADITION)

INTERCESSION

*T*HE MOVEMENT of prayer that brought you through petition, from dwelling on the past to committing to the future, in due course turns your face outward to all the other inhabitants of the divinely sustained universe. You realize that living for God and your own growth toward eternity impels you to profound concern for people you know and relate to. Your own well-being and development clearly depend on their conditions and circumstances. You cannot move forward in prayer and get closer to the divine when you sense their plight. You are challenged to put their needs before your own and to bring them before the divine in prayer. Even as you do so, you feel drawn to widen your area of concern.

The more you think about those known to you personally, the more you sense a responsibility for those beyond your horizons of both time and place. You feel for the plight of those suffering in distant parts of the world. You develop a strong sense of responsibility for those yet to be born who will inherit the world you have had a share in forming.

As the universe of your concern grows ever bigger, do not despair that you have control over such a tiny fragment of it. This broadening vision of commitment, the desire to pray for others and eventually for your enemies and those who have no sense of the sacred, is one of the clearest signs of spiritual growth. Pray for others because they need your prayer. Pray for yourself that you will know the needs of others and not be deaf to the cries of the needy. This is the golden rule of prayer.

Prayer itself will teach you the power of prayer as you find your caring heart growing in love not just for humankind but beyond, to the world of animals and nature, to a profound sense of responsibility for every aspect of the planet.

May everyone be happy,
May everyone be free from misery,
may no one ever be separated from their happiness,
May everyone have equanimity,
free from hatred and attachment.

(FROM THE BUDDHIST TRADITION)
GESHE KELSANG GYATSO AND MANJUSHRI CENTER, 1990/1996

May the merit generated through this practice be dedicated to the
enlightenment of all sentient beings.

(FROM THE BUDDHIST TRADITION)

All the people, like the vast expanse of the heavens,
are related to each other.
I pray that now and always you may bring them to liberation.

(FROM THE BUDDHIST TRADITION)

Be my protector, be my shield, with all who hold you dear.
The poor man's friend, the tyrant's foe, the strength of all this world.

(FROM THE SIKH TRADITION)

O Lord, answer us in the day of trouble,

Send us help from your holy place.

Show us the path of life,

For in your presence is joy.

Give justice to the orphan and oppressed

And break the power of wickedness and evil.

Look upon the hungry and sorrowful

And grant them the help for which they long.

Let the heavens rejoice and the ear be glad;

May your glory endure forever.

(FROM THE JUDEO-CHRISTIAN TRADITION)
THE EUROPEAN PROVINCE OF THE SOCIETY OF SAINT FRANCIS, 1992

THANKSGIVING

HE JOURNEY that is prayer begins with a sense of awe and wonder as you encounter and experience the divine in your life. It takes you through territory where you encounter the needs of other people and the many challenges facing the planet. Most of all, it brings you to a new knowledge of yourself as a partner called to work with the sacred power of the universe. But this journey has no end in this life. The destination is not a point in time at the end of a line or at the closing of a circle. The spiritual path can be thought of as a spiral. The route continues ever onward through territory that is familiar yet different. Your experience grows and you are better equipped for the challenges that lie ahead, yet there is always something new to discover.

The image of the spiral also reminds you that prayer is not an escape from the realities of the world and your obligations toward it, for moving on always means revisiting where you have been before and coming to terms with its meaning for you. What you first saw as a failing or a wrong to be confessed appears again as a diversion that led to a positive outcome, a crisis that became an opportunity. What you were once ashamed of in your past—poverty or lack of education, for example—appears in a new light as a way of coming close to those you can really help on their way. What you were once proud of— a business success or sporting achievement—turns out to have filled you with a set of values that blinded you to your real desire for spiritual growth.

As prayer deepens it is transformed. Awe and wonder turn to happiness and joy as the distance between you and the divine diminishes. Praise turns into thanksgiving, but these words hardly express what some experience as a time of great vitality, even ecstasy. This is what is meant by the mystical, the moment when prayer ceases to be something you do and becomes what you are.

I will give thanks to you, O Lord, with my whole heart;
before the gods will I sing praise to you.

I will bow down toward your holy temple and praise your name,
because of your love and faithfulness;
for you have glorified your name
and your word above all things.

In the day that I called to you, you answered me;
you put new strength in my soul.

All the kings of the earth shall praise you, O Lord,
for they have heard the words of your mouth.

They shall sing of the ways of the Lord,
that great is the glory of the Lord.

PSALM 138: 1–5 *(FROM THE JUDEO-CHRISTIAN TRADITION)*
COMMON WORSHIP, THE ARCHBISHOPS' COUNCIL, 2000

O Lord of All, all things creating,
O Self of All, all works performing,
O self at peace, Hidden mystery;
O Sun,
O Moon,
O Earth,
All hail to thee, for all that is.

FROM *THE MAITRI UPANISHAD*
(FROM THE HINDU TRADITION)

FURTHER READING

BRAYBROOKE, M. *Learning to Pray: A Practical Guide to Enriching Your Life Through Prayer.* Duncan Baird, UK, 2001.

WALKER, A. *Prayer For Everyday Living.* Godsfield Press, UK, 2003.

ACKNOWLEDGMENTS

The publishers would like to thank the following for permission to reproduce copyright material:

CORBIS IMAGES: pp. 1 Paul Edmondson; 10/11 Macduff Everton; 15 Najlah Feanny-Hicks; 17 Michael Freeman; 28 Tom Nebbia; 30 Bryan F. Peterson; 36 Annie Griffiths Belt; 37 Jonathan Blair; 39 Kelly-Mooney; 43 Lindsay Hebberd; 47 Reza; 49 Carl Purcell; 52 Peter Turnley; 54/55 Farrell Grehan; 62 Anthony Redpath; 65 Lindsay Hebbard; 67 Arthur Thevenart; 78 David Muench; 81 Blake Woken; 82 David Turnley; 87 Galen Rowell; 88 Peter Turnley; 96 Randy Wells.

STEPHEN FRANCIS: p. 91